THE OFFICIAL
LIVERPOOL FC
ANNUAL 2010

YOU'LL NEVER WALK ALONE

LIVERPOOL
FOOTBALL CLUB

EST·1892 ®

Written By Paul Eaton

Designed By Alice Lake-Hammond

A Grange Publication

© 2009. Published by Grange Communications Ltd., Edinburgh, under licence from Liverpool Football Club. Printed in the EU.

Photographs © David Rawcliffe/Propaganda & Press Association Images
Liverpool FC logo and crest are registered trademarks of The Liverpool Football Club and Athletic Grounds Ltd.

ISBN: 978-1-906211-82-0

£6.99

Contents

Introduction 5

Season Review 6

Rafael Benitez Interview 14

Season Quiz 18

Steven Gerrard Interview 20

Hyypia Tribute 24

Fernando Torres 28

The Kop Comes to Asia 34

Dirk Kuyt Interview 36

Academy 38

Glen Johnson 40

Alberto Aquilani 42

Spot the Ball 46

Spot the Difference 47

Daniel Agger Interview 48

LFC Records 50

Pepe Reina Interview 52

LFC in 50 Quotes 54

Albert Riera Interview 56

Lucas Leiva Interview 58

Quiz Answers 60

Introduction

Liverpool Football Club reached their highest ever Barclays Premier League points total in the 2008/09 season with 86 points, and finished 2nd despite only losing 2 games all season.

In this year's Annual we reflect on the season that saw the Reds finish as the League's top scorers with 77 goals - the highest goals per game average of any team in the top four divisions in England. Along the way we ended Chelsea's 86-game unbeaten home record and recorded our biggest win at Old Trafford in 72 years, beating Manchester United 4-1. Our 4-0 defeat of Real Madrid in the UEFA Champions League was another highlight to remember.

The 2010 Annual also recaps each of Fernando Torres' first 50 goals for Liverpool FC - a feat he achieved in just two seasons. We also have interviews with Rafa Benitez, Steven Gerrard, Dirk Kuyt, Glen Johnson and more.

Enjoy the read!

AUGUST

After a goalless draw in the first leg of their Champions League qualifier against Standard Liege, Liverpool FC kicked off their domestic season by picking up three points at Sunderland thanks to a late Fernando Torres strike. An even later net-buster brought three points the following week as Steven Gerrard ensured the Reds began their Anfield campaign with a victory - his stoppage time winner against Middlesbrough signalling a sign of things to come as far as Liverpool FC and last-minute winners were concerned.

Dirk Kuyt was the scorer of our most important goal of the month as his last-gasp injury time goal finally broke the deadlock in the return with Liege, and ensured the Reds' place in the group stages of the Champions League. The month ended with a hard fought point at Villa Park as the Reds held the home side to a goalless draw.

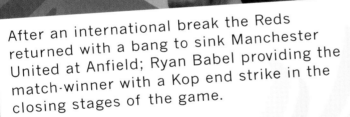

SEPTEMBER

After an international break the Reds returned with a bang to sink Manchester United at Anfield; Ryan Babel providing the match-winner with a Kop end strike in the closing stages of the game.

The Champions League group stages kicked off in the south of France as Steven Gerrard scored a glorious goal to help take three points from Marseille, but back at Anfield the following weekend Stoke City frustrated the home side and left Merseyside with a point to show for their efforts.

Our Carling Cup campaign kicked off with a home victory over Crewe - but a much tougher test awaited at the weekend when we took the short trip to Goodison for the first derby of the season. Fernando Torres was the derby day hero with two second half goals to secure local bragging rights for the red half of the city.

PSV Eindhoven were comfortably defeated at Anfield as our European campaign gathered momentum. Steven Gerrard was among the scorers on the night to register his 100th goal for the Reds in all competitions. Manchester City and then Wigan both took us to five goal thrillers in the next two matches, with Dirk Kuyt netting an injury time goal to take the points at Eastlands while the Dutchman was again on hand to sink the Latics late on after Wigan had twice led at Anfield.

October 26 is a date Chelsea fans are unlikely to forget in a hurry as we became the first team to win at Stamford Bridge in the league for more than 80 games - Xabi Alonso's first half strike proving the difference on the day. With confidence sky high, Portsmouth were next on the receiving end as Steven Gerrard's penalty secured all three points in the night-time clash at Anfield. Meanwhile, in Europe, Robbie Keane's goal helped take a point from Madrid against Fernando Torres' former Atletico team.

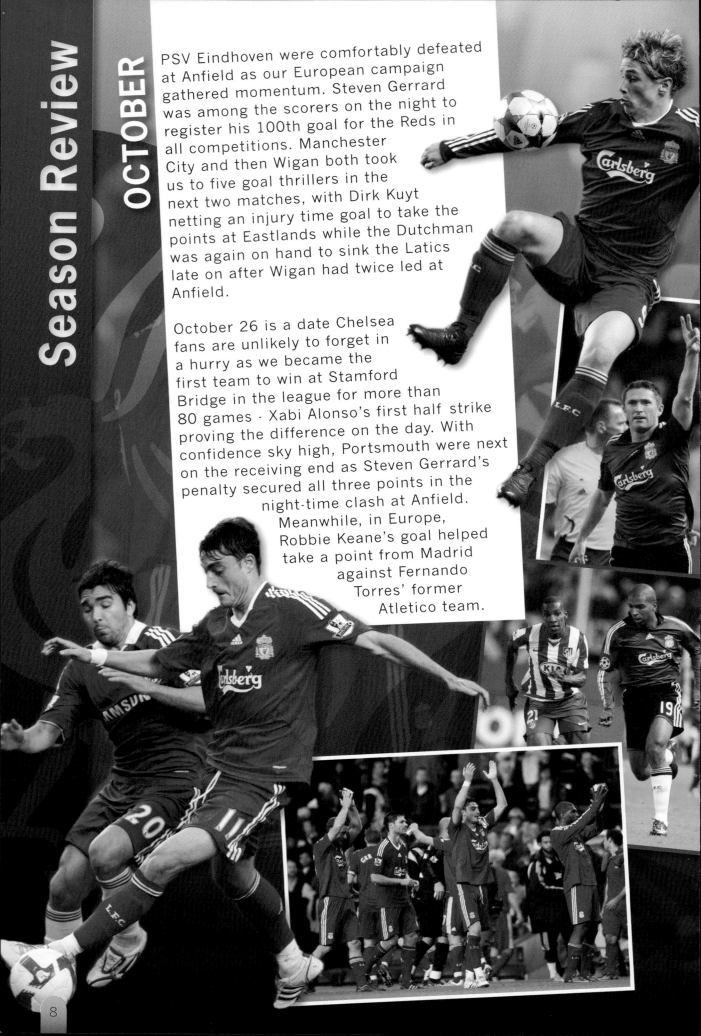

NOVEMBER

Our first defeat of the campaign arrived on the first day of the month as we let a lead slip at Tottenham, eventually going down to a 2-1 defeat despite it being one of our best away performances of the season. Tottenham would also knock us out of the Carling Cup later in the month, but we continued to perform well in both the league and Europe with West Brom routed at Anfield and another important Champions League point being earned against Atletico thanks to Steven Gerrard's late penalty.

Dirk Kuyt and Steven Gerrard scored in a 2-0 victory over Bolton while the Reds hit the top of the table the following week, despite the clear disappointment of only taking a point from a goalless draw with Fulham at Anfield. Gerrard was on the scoresheet again in our final game of the month, netting the only goal of the game in a 1-0 victory over Olympique Marseille as we began to take control of our qualifying group.

DECEMBER

West Ham became the latest side to take a point at Anfield when they held the Reds to a goalless draw. The Reds were continuing to impress on the road as a 3-1 victory at Blackburn proved the following week. Our Champions League group campaign was concluded with a 3-1 victory in Eindhoven, but back at Anfield a point was dropped as Hull ran into a 2-0 lead before being pegged back to 2-2.

Robbie Keane was on target at Arsenal as we took an excellent point from the Emirates, and the year ended in great style as Bolton were comfortably defeated on Boxing Day before we went goal crazy at Newcastle to send the Magpies crashing to a 5-1 defeat, which could have been many more on the day.

JANUARY

A new year brought the start of a new competition, and FA Cup progress was secured at Preston thanks to goals in each half from Albert Riera and Fernando Torres, with the Spanish striker back fit again after a lengthy lay-off. January would prove to be a tough month for the Reds in the league, with Stoke City and Everton taking a point each away from Anfield, while in the FA Cup Everton again frustrated us as we were held to a 1-1 draw and had to contend with a Goodison replay. Things didn't get any better three days later as Wigan netted a late penalty to deny us all three points at the JJB.

FEBRUARY

A new month brought new fortune and the league double was brilliantly completed over Chelsea thanks to two late Fernando Torres goals at Anfield.

But the FA Cup proved to be a different story as Everton snatched a late injury time winner to send us out of the competition at the fourth round stage. Off to the south coast we went looking for an instant response at Portsmouth, and it looked for so long as though more precious points were going to be lost until Torres converted a close range header to secure victory in the dying stages of the game. It was yet another Liverpool FC late-show.

Sadly, Manchester City were able to earn a 1-1 draw at Anfield in our next outing, but just a few days later Yossi Benayoun headed home a famous winner in the Bernabeu to give us a 1-0 lead over Real Madrid to bring back to Anfield for the return leg of the Champions League last sixteen clash.

The last match of the month saw the Reds' second league defeat to Middlesbrough at the Riverside the next weekend.

After a straightforward 2-0 victory over Sunderland, Liverpool FC fans enjoyed a dream week with famous victories over both Manchester United and Real Madrid. Firstly, Madrid had no answer to Liverpool FC's stunning display at Anfield as we rattled home four goals without reply to set up a quarter-final date with Chelsea. It would be the fifth season in a row we had faced the Londoners in Europe. Then Manchester United were crushed 4-1 at Old Trafford thanks to goals from Fernando Torres, Steven Gerrard, Fabio Aurelio and Andrea Dossena.

With the players and fans buoyant, it came as no surprise to see another goal-fest in our next outing, this time Aston Villa being taken apart and demolished 5-0 in one of the most one-sided games of the season.

MANCHESTER UNITED 1 2:40
LIVERPOOL 4 0:00

LIVERPOOL 5
VILLA 0

11

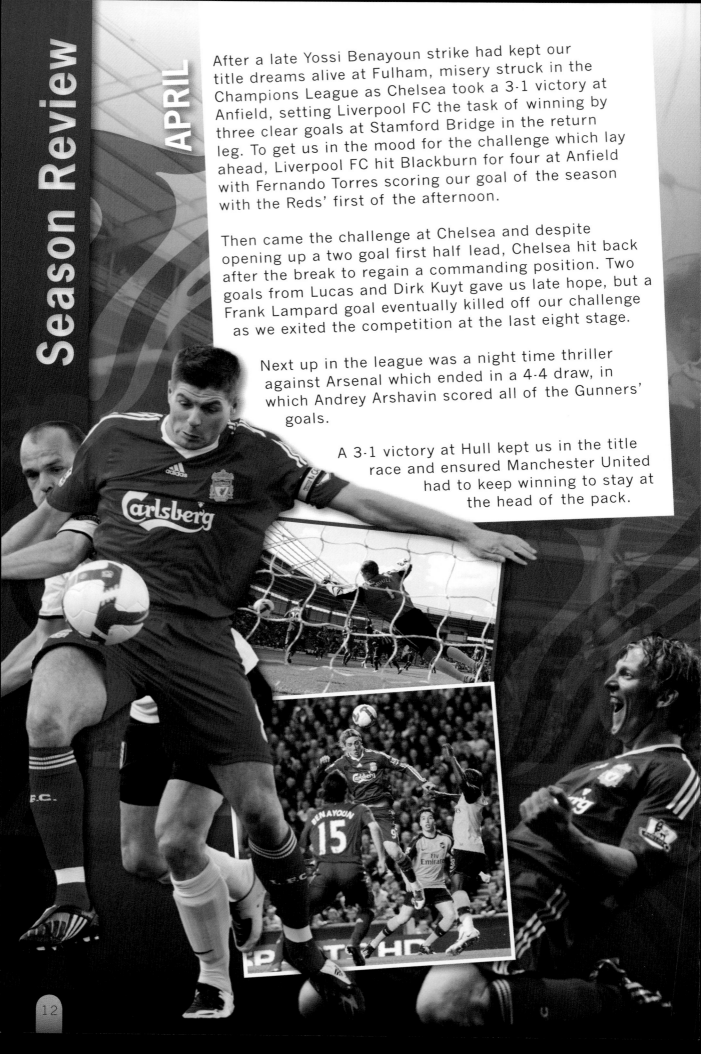

After a late Yossi Benayoun strike had kept our title dreams alive at Fulham, misery struck in the Champions League as Chelsea took a 3-1 victory at Anfield, setting Liverpool FC the task of winning by three clear goals at Stamford Bridge in the return leg. To get us in the mood for the challenge which lay ahead, Liverpool FC hit Blackburn for four at Anfield with Fernando Torres scoring our goal of the season with the Reds' first of the afternoon.

Then came the challenge at Chelsea and despite opening up a two goal first half lead, Chelsea hit back after the break to regain a commanding position. Two goals from Lucas and Dirk Kuyt gave us late hope, but a Frank Lampard goal eventually killed off our challenge as we exited the competition at the last eight stage.

Next up in the league was a night time thriller against Arsenal which ended in a 4-4 draw, in which Andrey Arshavin scored all of the Gunners' goals.

A 3-1 victory at Hull kept us in the title race and ensured Manchester United had to keep winning to stay at the head of the pack.

MAY

Liverpool FC recorded four straight victories in May over Newcastle, West Ham, West Brom and Tottenham, with eleven goals being scored and only one conceded. However, it wasn't to be enough as United won the league by four points and we had to be content with second place.

The final game of the season against Spurs at Anfield was notable for both Sami Hyypia's farewell after ten years as a Liverpool FC player and Fernando Torres' opening goal in the game which took him to 50 goals in just two years for Liverpool FC.

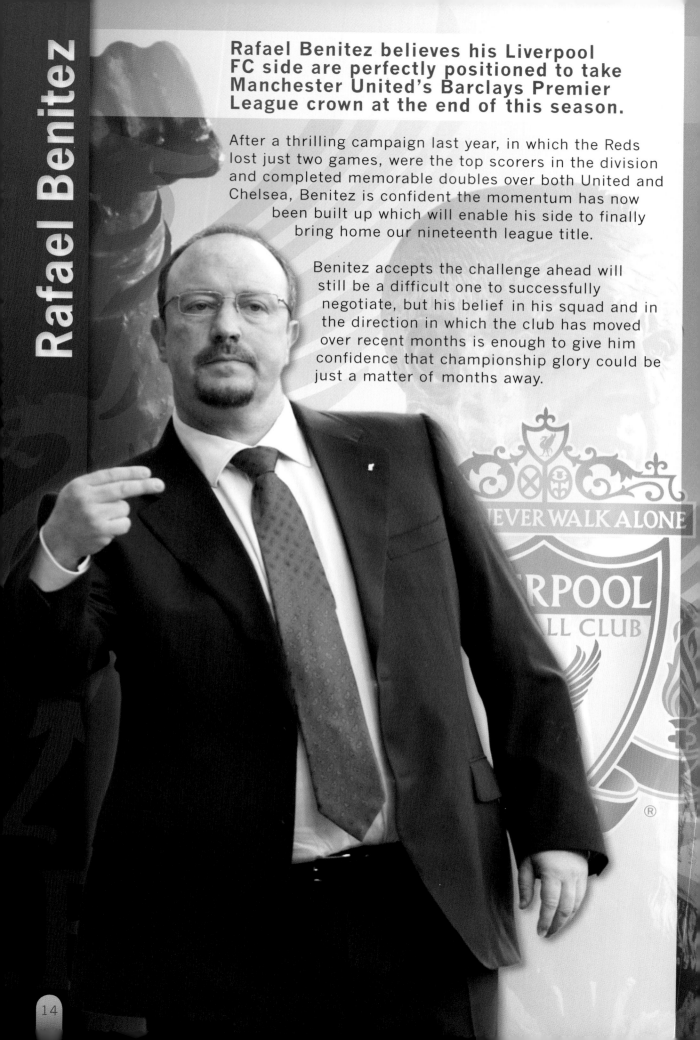

Rafael Benitez

Rafael Benitez believes his Liverpool FC side are perfectly positioned to take Manchester United's Barclays Premier League crown at the end of this season.

After a thrilling campaign last year, in which the Reds lost just two games, were the top scorers in the division and completed memorable doubles over both United and Chelsea, Benitez is confident the momentum has now been built up which will enable his side to finally bring home our nineteenth league title.

Benitez accepts the challenge ahead will still be a difficult one to successfully negotiate, but his belief in his squad and in the direction in which the club has moved over recent months is enough to give him confidence that championship glory could be just a matter of months away.

"Clearly we have improved and are continuing to make progress," said the Liverpool FC manager. "We have got better every year we have been here and everyone can see we progressed last season.

"We didn't know everything when we first arrived here. Now we can see little things that can make a massive difference.

"Now we know these things we can be more precise, sign players in a better way, approach games and different competitions in a better way. We know the rules and the style of the game in England much better now.

"Maybe sometimes you don't need as long to start challenging as it has taken us. But when the other teams are so strong it becomes much more difficult. You can try to move fast, but if they go as fast as you, you have to go faster.

"The only way to do that is to try to sign the right players every single time.

"With Sami Hyypia leaving we have just two players left at the club from when I took over - Steven Gerrard and Jamie Carragher.

"Coming to a club that needs a lot of work is a massive difference to arriving at a club without too many changes to make. From my time here, Chelsea and United already had big squads with top-class players. They have both spent big money since and improved a lot.

"We could not spend that kind of money, but look at the level of the squad now compared to five years ago. We have had to work hard rebuilding the whole squad.

"It's not just a case of saying, 'Oh, Liverpool should win because they are spending.' The other clubs are spending too but had better squads from the beginning. That is why if we are to reduce the gap we have to do things almost perfectly.

"We have learned together what it means to stay close to the top of the table from the beginning to the end. I am sure that will help us in the future."

Benitez's confidence is largely based on the impressive spine which runs throughout his team - and one which probably cannot be bettered anywhere in the English game.

"We know where we need to improve and hopefully we can work as hard this year and keep moving in the right direction."

"We have Pepe Reina as the number one goalkeeper with Diego Cavalieri behind him, another good goalkeeper. Then we have Skrtel, Carragher and Agger - three good centre-backs," he added.

"Then you go to the midfield with Alonso, Mascherano, Lucas and Gerrard, with Torres up front and Ngog, who is a very good prospect. We have a good squad that is still young, so hopefully we can improve further."

Whatever the preferred line-up for the Reds this season, it goes without saying the fitness of star duo Steven Gerrard and Fernando Torres will be key to our chances of silverware.

Having started just 12 out of 38 games together in the league last season, Benitez is conscious of the need for that statistic to be improved this time around.

"We have a squad full of good players, but when Torres and Gerrard are on the pitch you know the opposition will be more worried," he said.

"They are quality players who can win matches in a second. It's a pity they weren't fit for more games last season because I am sure we could have picked up more points if they'd been involved in more games.

"But a positive for me is we have shown we can win games whoever is in the side. When we had injuries last year the quality of the squad was tested and it was pleasing to see other players coming in and doing a job. We won some big games last year without Stevie and Torres and that can only be a good thing. Clearly, though, it is better if they are fit and playing."

It seems all the superlatives have been said and written about Gerrard's form over recent months. His best ever season last year in terms of goals scored was rewarded when the Football Writers voted him as their Footballer of the Year, but as far as his manager is concerned there is still room for improvement.

"He has learnt a lot, and he is still keen to learn," said his manager.

"If you analyse his numbers - he's scored 23, 11, 21 and now 24. I remember when we talked about him as a right winger and everyone was talking in the press, but he still got 23 that year.

"Now in a free role he got 24, which is a fantastic achievement for him. I was really pleased because he said it was thanks to his team-mates - that is really positive.

"Hopefully he can improve even more next year. He knows the position a little bit but he is aware that he can still improve. There are one or two little things that if he works on he will be even better."

"We have learned together what it means to stay close to the top of the table from the beginning to the end. I am sure that will help us in the future."

Despite an impressive 86 points not being enough to win the title last term, Benitez believes that total is still one worth aiming for this time around.

"For sure I would have taken 86 points at the start and I would also have been sure that we'd have won something with this amount of points but the Premier League is very strong, it's always difficult.

"It was good but you cannot say 'success' if you don't win a trophy.

"Two or three of the top sides in the world are in England, so clearly it's not easy to win trophies.

"But to break some records, score a lot of goals and not concede many, and to only lose two games is not bad.

"Clearly, if you analyse the numbers to see why we have improved, there are two or three things. But the main one is the results against the top four.

"Also, our results away have been much better. At home we can talk about the figures and the draws - but more or less it was the same as the season before.

"We know where we need to improve and hopefully we can work as hard this year and keep moving in the right direction."

1 From which club did Liverpool FC sign Fernando Torres?

What squad number does Pepe Reina wear? **2**

3 Who did Liverpool FC defeat on the last day of last season?

Who made his farewell appearance for Liverpool FC on that afternoon? **4**

5 What nationality is Fabio Aurelio?

In which year was Liverpool Football Club formed? **6**

7 Who was Liverpool FC manager before Rafael Benitez?

Who did Liverpool FC beat in the 1978 European Cup final? **8**

9 In which city was the 1981 European Cup final played?

Who are Liverpool FC's shirt sponsors? **10**

11 Lucas joined Liverpool FC from which Brazilian club?

12 How many goals did Steven Gerrard score last season?

13 Who is Liverpool FC's reserve team manager?

14 And who has taken over as Academy Manager?

15 What nationality is Academy youngster Lauri Dalla Valle?

16 What squad number does Jamie Carragher wear?

17 Steven Gerrard scored his 100th goal for Liverpool FC against which side?

18 Who scored Liverpool FC's goal at Anfield against Chelsea in the Champions League last season?

19 Who knocked Liverpool FC out of last season's Carling Cup?

20 Which goal was voted Liverpool FC's Goal of the Season for 2008/09?

Answers P.60

He may have ended last season as the Football Writers' choice as their Player of the Year, but Steven Gerrard has insisted he will gladly swap any personal honours for league championship glory.

The Liverpool FC captain deservedly won the vote of the country's top football journalists as their star performer last term, as Liverpool FC ran Manchester United to within the penultimate weekend of the season in the title race.

It was ultimately a forlorn race as far as the Reds were concerned as Manchester United fended off the challenge of Rafael Benitez's men to secure the top prize, but Gerrard has seen enough over the past twelve months to convince him Liverpool FC are closer than ever to a nineteenth title success.

"I was really proud of the boys last season," he said. "It was the first time I've ever been involved in a title race and, from a personal point of view, I've certainly enjoyed it. Speaking to the other boys, they've enjoyed it too.

"Obviously we were unfortunate not to win the league, but we can take a lot of positives from the season moving forward.

"We've put in some terrific performances and have performed well as a team. I think we can use this experience and take big confidence into the future.

"As far as trophies are concerned, we've finished empty handed, but I think we can be really proud of how we have performed. From maybe mid-December onwards we've shown Championship winning form.

"To win the Premier League you have to have had experience of being involved in a title race and let's hope the experience we've gained this year will help us go one better next season."

On reflection, while enjoying memorable doubles over both Manchester United and Chelsea, Gerrard admits lost points at home ultimately proved costly as the team made mistakes which he hopes are learned from in the new campaign.

"Looking back at those three draws on the spin at home in December, they're key because if we had turned them into wins, we'd probably be champions or at least still in the race with one game to go," he reflected.

"But that shows everyone how difficult this league is to win and that you need to perform immaculately at home and win all your games.

"To finish with 86 points was still a fantastic achievement.

"I think we can take belief from going to Old Trafford, Stamford Bridge and the Emirates and remaining unbeaten.

"If we can take that confidence and belief into those games next season and perform in the same way, as well as turning the home draws into wins, I think we could be champions."

"We've put in some terrific performances and have performed well as a team. I think we can use this experience and take big confidence into the future."

And as a boyhood fan of the club himself, Gerrard admits he wants to win the title for the fans as much as for himself.

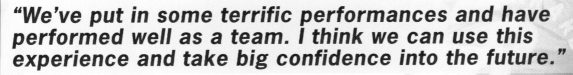

"I think the supporters deserve it," he added. "They have given us terrific support once again over the course of the season.

"They've stuck with us all the way through and we know how much they want to win that trophy. It's a dream shared by us all. We all want to win it. It means so much to everyone connected with the club and hopefully we can achieve it next season."

And as far as his Footballer of the Year trophy was concerned, Gerrard insists he owes a debt of gratitude to many people who helped him win one of the game's most prestigious honours.

"When you look at the quality of the players there are in this league, it's a great privilege to win this kind of award," he said.

"It's made even more special for me because I am following in the footsteps of Liverpool players like John Barnes, Steve Nicol and Kenny Dalglish who were heroes of mine.

"Then further back players like Ian Callaghan and Terry McDermott who were heroes to my dad and so many other Liverpool fans.

"It's not just the Manchester United players - when you look at the players the likes of Chelsea and Arsenal and other teams have got, they all have fantastic players throughout their squads now.

"The quality is getting better and better each year so to win this award is a great achievement for myself.

"But I've had fantastic help along the way from everyone at this football club.

"My family and friends come every time I play and everything I achieve in football they are a very big part of because they are there for me 24 hours a day, seven days a week.

"But the biggest thank yous have to go to the manager, the coaching staff and my team-mates.

"Individual awards are great but you don't win them without great help from those people."

"If we can take that confidence and belief into those games next season and perform in the same way ... I think we could be champions."

After ten years of outstanding service at Anfield, Sami Hyypia finally said goodbye to the Liverpool FC fans on the final day of last season against Tottenham at Anfield.

The Finnish international - arguably one of the greatest foreigners ever to play in this country - rejected the Reds' offer of a new contract in favour of a move to German side Bayer Leverkusen, with the opportunity to play more regular first team football central to his decision to quit Anfield.

Kopites gave him a rousing send-off during the final day victory over Spurs, with Hyypia clearly shedding tears as he was lofted high by his team-mates as the players completed their traditional end of season lap of honour.

"I still think I'm young enough to play football and I know chances to play here would be limited," he said. "I spoke to the manager and I didn't want him to make promises about how many games I would play, but this season has been mentally very difficult. I haven't played a lot and playing is what I enjoy most.

"I understand it isn't possible to play enough games here for me to be happy, so I had to look elsewhere. I got the option to go abroad to Bayer Leverkusen. The whole package was good, they have big plans for me and hopefully I can go there and help them to be successful.

"From day one I have felt at home here. I have had good relationships with the club, with the staff and all the players who have been here over the last ten years. It's difficult to leave but my reasons are all professional. I still want to play football.

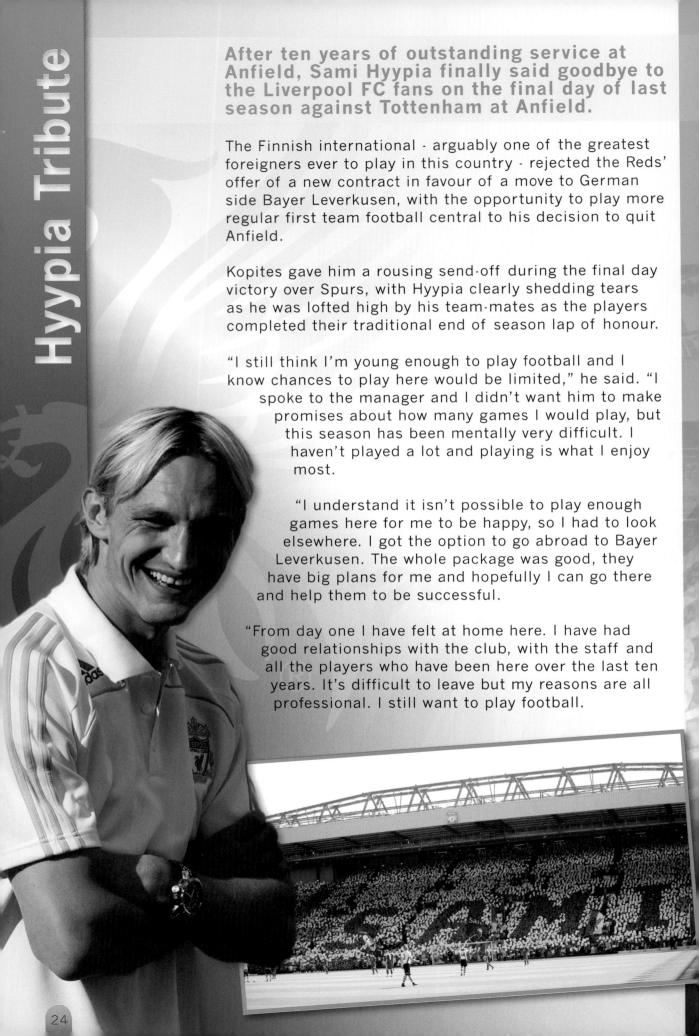

"Ten years is a long time to spend at one club. My family are settled here and I know it will be stressful moving with them into a new house in a new country. But the professional side drove this decision. It's a new challenge and I will give it everything to be successful in Germany."

While everybody at Anfield wishes Sami the best of luck in his new career, it's worth reflecting on his ten magnificent years at Anfield and selecting his top 3 moments in a Liverpool FC shirt.

The Juventus volley

Having been relegated to the bench for the previous three league games, Sami returned to the starting line-up in place of the ineligible Mauricio Pellegrino for the visit of Italian giants Juventus.

"He is a brilliant professional and he's been a big player for such a long time with Liverpool ... he leads by example and never lets them down."

Many observers felt the Turin side would prove too strong for Rafael Benitez's hopefuls, but Liverpool FC thought otherwise and duly set about ripping up the form book. A supercharged start proved to be the key to winning the quarter-final tie and it was Sami who broke the deadlock in sensational style.

The Reds had already gone close through Milan Baros when Luis Garcia flicked on Steven Gerrard's right-wing corner for Hyypia to arrive and steer a fine volley beyond Gianluigi Buffon on 10 minutes.

It was the perfect way to return to the starting line-up and when Garcia doubled the advantage 15 minutes later Liverpool FC looked set for the last four.

However, a second-half header from Fabio Cannavaro gave the visitors hope and Sami and co had to be at their defensive best in the second-leg to earn the goalless draw that secured a semi-final with Chelsea.

Speaking later that year Sami admitted it had been one of the highlights of his season.

"That goal was something special for me and it gave us a good lift for that game," he said. "Luis scored another great goal as well.

"Like I say, it was a special night for me."

The miracle of Istanbul

For all the success of the treble season, Istanbul will always be the highlight of Sami's 10 year stay at Anfield.

To win the Champions League is to reach the pinnacle of your profession for most footballers, and yet, at half-time it was looking like being THE low point for Sami and co.

The Reds trailed AC Milan by three goals and had been left chasing shadows in what was a torrid 45 minutes for the men from Merseyside.

However, the scoreboard could have read very differently had Sami's towering header from Steven Gerrard's cross found the corner of Dida's net with the score still at 1-0.

Unfortunately it wasn't to be for the Finn. A reshuffle at the break saw Djimi Traore join Sami and Carra as part of a three man defence and within 15 minutes of the restart Liverpool FC had produced a miracle to draw level.

It was fairytale stuff and just like his fellow defenders, Hyypia would play an important role in keeping Milan at bay as the Reds began to tire.

Indeed, he was on hand to clear a dangerous header back across goal in stoppage time to ensure the Reds made it safely through to extra-time.

With concentration levels wilting, Liverpool FC's defence managed to hold firm throughout the extended period to see the match through to penalties where the Reds went on to claim victory and secure the fifth European Cup in our history.

"I think it's much better than 2001 and the amount of people that have come out to see us is just fantastic," he recalled. "It really is unbelievable and I don't know whether to laugh or cry.

"It is a great achievement and I am still wondering just what we have done. This is a great thing in my career and I now have a Champions League winners medal.

"The way we came back from 3-0 down shows you the character of this team and it is just one of the best days of my life. I hope we can win many more trophies for these fantastic supporters."

Rolling back the years - the 4-1 thumping of United

Sami rolled back the years with a virtuoso performance at Old Trafford that will arguably go down as Liverpool FC's best league victory in living memory.

What makes Hyypia's outstanding display even more astonishing is the fact he did not know he was playing until seconds before kick-off.

An injury to Alvaro Arbeloa forced a defensive reshuffle and the Finn was drafted into the starting XI at the eleventh hour.

One particular left-footed touch saw him pluck the ball from the air inside his own penalty area. It was just one of the great moments on an unforgettable afternoon for the Reds and capped a sensational four day period, following the 4-0 rout of Real Madrid.

"It's been a good week," said Hyypia after the game. "I was just asked if I've had a week like this before and I couldn't think of one since in 2001 when we won a few cups in one week."

When asked about his impressive display following his late inclusion in the starting line-up his response was typically modest.

"I found out just a few minutes before we came out," he said.

"I was wondering how the first minutes would go but I got into it and had no problems."

Hyypia's performance quite rightly drew countless plaudits, with the legendary Alan Hansen summing up his contribution perfectly.

"He is a brilliant professional and he's been a big player for such a long time with Liverpool," he said. "He leads by example and never lets them down."

"From day one I have felt at home here. I have had good relationships with the club, with the staff and all the players who have been here over the last ten years."

Fernando Torres' final goal of the 2008/09 season took his tally as a Liverpool FC player to an incredible 50 in just two seasons at Anfield.

To celebrate this marvellous achievement, we've compiled a list of every one of El Nino's strikes and, as you can see from reading the list below, he's already endeared himself to Kopites all over the world with some never-to-be-forgotten net-busters.

1 Chelsea   Barclays Premier League   19 Aug 2007
Latching on to a piercing Steven Gerrard through-ball, the Reds' new signing glided past Chelsea defender Tal Ben-Haim before dispatching a low shot beyond Petr Cech into the bottom corner.

2 Derby County   Barclays Premier League   1 Sept 2007
He left the opposition defenders for dead and slotted the ball into the bottom corner via his left boot in the 56th minute.

3 Derby County   Barclays Premier League   1 Sept 2007
Derby defender Andy Todd failed to deal with Andriy Voronin's lobbed ball forward, allowing Torres to go through on goal, effortlessly round goalkeeper Stephen Bywater and slide the ball into an empty net.

4 Reading   Carling Cup third round   25 Sept 2007
Torres marked his return to Liverpool FC's starting line-up with a memorable hat-trick at the Madejski Stadium.
His first came early in the second half as Sebastian Leto's pass sent the Spanish international through on goal. El Nino held off the advances of Reading defender Andre Bikey before dispatching a low shot into the bottom corner.

5 Reading
Carling Cup third round   25 Sept 2007
His second of the evening arrived in the 72nd minute. John Arne Riise's cut-back from the byline found Torres, who opened up his body brilliantly to turn the ball into the far corner from 12-yards.

6 Reading
Carling Cup third round   25 Sept 2007
Torres completed his first hat-trick in English football as he collected a Steven Gerrard through ball, leaving the defence trailing in his wake, before nonchalantly rounding Reading goalkeeper Adam Federici to cap a wonderful night for the Reds' record signing.

7 Tottenham Hotspur
Barclays Premier League   7 Oct 2007
It looked as though the three points were heading to White Hart Lane until Torres headed home Steve Finnan's deep cross to salvage a point for Liverpool FC in stoppage-time.

El Nino left Aaron Hughes floundering before calmly beating Antti Niemi with a clever reverse shot into the bottom corner from 10 yards.

8 Fulham   Barclays Premier League   10 Nov 2007

Torres came off the bench to score a brilliant individual goal to break Fulham's resistance and put Liverpool FC on their way to three points. The Spaniard chested down Pepe Reina's long goal-kick before turning and running at the Fulham defence. El Nino left Aaron Hughes floundering before calmly beating Antti Niemi with a clever reverse shot into the bottom corner from 10 yards.

9 FC Porto   Champions League group stage   28 Nov 2007

His first Champions League goal came early in the first half as Torres escaped the attention of two Porto defenders to plant a downward header into the back of the net from Steven Gerrard's corner.

10 FC Porto Champions League group stage   28 Nov 2007

Collecting Harry Kewell's pass, Liverpool FC's number nine turned his marker inside the box before curling a shot into the far corner of the goal to send Anfield into raptures.

11 Bolton Wanderers
Barclays Premier League   2 Dec 2007

Steven Gerrard was the provider as his long pass sliced open the Bolton defence, sending Torres through on goal and the Spaniard deftly lifted the ball over the advancing Jussi Jaaskelainen.

12 Marseille
Champions League   11 Dec 2007

Torres netted the second in a must-win game; after collecting Harry Kewell's pass on the left edge of the area, he bamboozled the Marseille defence with a mazy run before calmly rolling the ball into the bottom corner.

13 Portsmouth
Barclays Premier League   22 Dec 2007

His first of the game came in the 67th minute when he calmly rolled the ball into the bottom corner after Pompey 'keeper David James had inadvertently deflected it into his path.

14 Portsmouth
Barclays Premier League   22 Dec 2007

Jamie Carragher's lofted ball into the area was headed back to Torres by Steven Gerrard and the striker clinically dispatched a left-footed volley into the bottom corner.

15 Derby County
Barclays Premier League   26 Dec 2007

Torres put the Reds ahead after 11 minutes with a festive cracker. Ryan Babel laid the ball off and the Spaniard burst into the box, nutmegging Darren Moore en route, before curling a shot into the far corner.

16 Wigan Athletic
Barclays Premier League   2 Jan 2008

A well worked move resulted in Steven Gerrard releasing Steve Finnan into the right hand channel and his low cross was turned past Chris Kirkland by El Nino from 10 yards.

17 - Middlesbrough Barclays Premier League   12 Jan 2008
With Liverpool FC trailing, Torres collected possession 25 yards from goal and ran at the Boro defence before drilling an unstoppable strike in off the post to earn the Reds a point.

18 - Sunderland   Barclays Premier League   2 Feb 2008
Peter Crouch's flick-on put Torres through on goal, and the end result was never in doubt as he slammed the ball past Craig Gordon.

19 - Middlesbrough Barclays Premier League   23 Feb 2008
Torres became the first Liverpool FC player to score 20 goals or more in a season since Michael Owen in 2002/03 with a treble against Middlesbrough. His first was something of a gift as Julio Arca's header towards his own goal on 28 minutes only succeeded in finding the lurking Torres and the Reds' number nine didn't need a second invitation to equalize.

20 Middlesbrough   Barclays Premier League   23 Feb 2008
The Spanish star claimed his second in as many minutes. This time, fed by Fabio Aurelio, he powered a low drive into the left corner from 25 yards.

21 Middlesbrough   Barclays Premier League   23 Feb 2008
Dirk Kuyt's cross-field pass drew Boro goalkeeper Mark Schwarzer to the edge of his area but Torres beat both him, and defender David Wheater, to the ball and lofted it into the unguarded goal.

22 West Ham United   Barclays Premier League   5 Mar 2008
He notched his first of the evening after just eight minutes when he got ahead of his marker to steer Dirk Kuyt's cross from the right past Robert Green with the side of his right boot.

23 West Ham United   Barclays Premier League   5 Mar 2008
This time the Dutchman's cross back into the area following a half-cleared Reds corner was precisely headed home from close-range by Torres.

...the first player in Liverpool FC history to net in seven successive top-flight games at Anfield.

24 West Ham United
Barclays Premier League 5 Mar 2008
Pouncing on to John Arne Riise's header into the box, the Reds' striker dinked the ball through the legs of the hapless Lucas Neill and steered it across the body of Robert Green into the bottom corner for league goal number 18 of his debut season at Anfield.

25 Newcastle United
Barclays Premier League 8 Mar 2008
Torres headed the ball down to Gerrard on the half-way line and the Reds' skipper charged at the Newcastle defence before playing an incisive pass into the run of our number nine. The Spaniard sold 'keeper Steve Harper an outrageous dummy and slid the ball into the back of the net for his 25th goal of the season.

26 Inter Milan **Champions League last 16 (2nd leg)** 11 Mar 2008
Fabio Aurelio's pass from the left found Torres on the edge of the area. In a flash, he spun his marker and dispatched a half-volley into the bottom corner with unerring accuracy.

27 Reading **Barclays Premier League** 15 Mar 2008
Torres reached the 20 league goals milestone against Reading. The Reds' number nine lost his marker to plant a firm header past Marcus Hahnemann to claim his ninth goal in six games.

28 Everton **Barclays Premier League** 30 Mar 2008
Xabi Alonso reclaimed possession on the edge of the Everton box after the Blues had attempted to clear from a corner and Dirk Kuyt flicked the ball into Torres' path inside the box. The outcome was inevitable as the Spaniard drilled low across the body of Tim Howard in front of the Kop.

29 Arsenal
Champions League quarter-final (2nd leg) 8 Apr 2008
Peter Crouch's flick-on found Torres just inside the box and he turned his marker in a heartbeat before firing home into the top corner to send the Kop into delirium early in the second half.

30 Blackburn Rovers
Barclays Premier League 13 Apr 2008
The landmarks continued to come for El Nino as he became the first player in Liverpool FC history to net in seven successive top-flight games at Anfield with a goal against Blackburn. It came eight minutes from time when he met a Steven Gerrard cross at the back post with a fine header to beat goalkeeper Brad Friedel.

31 Chelsea Champions League semi-final (2nd leg) 30 Apr 2008
Yossi Benayoun's jinking run saw him thread the ball through to Torres inside the box and the Spaniard kept his cool under pressure to sweep a low shot past Petr Cech.

32 Manchester City **Barclays Premier League** 4 May 2008
Torres' electric pace left City defender Richard Dunne for dead before the striker slipped the ball into the far corner of the goal.

33 Tottenham Hotspur **Barclays Premier League** 11 May 2008
Torres netted his 24th league goal of the season to beat Ruud van Nistelrooy's record for most league goals by a foreigner in a debut season in English football. The goal came in the 74th minute when the striker turned a Tottenham defender inside out before sliding the ball under the body of Spurs 'keeper Radek Cerny.

34 Sunderland   Barclays Premier League   16 Aug 2008
With the game heading for a draw, the Spanish striker picked up Xabi Alonso's pass and lashed a ferocious shot into the bottom corner from 25-yards to secure the three points.

35 Everton   Barclays Premier League   27 Sept 2008
Torres struck twice in three minutes to secure a 2-0 victory for Liverpool FC, with the first goal coming on 59 minutes when the Spaniard ghosted in at the far post to deftly volley Robbie Keane's cross through the legs of Tim Howard.

36 Everton   Barclays Premier League   27 Sept 2008
Torres added his, and Liverpool FC's, second within minutes of his first when he showed his predatory instincts by pouncing on a loose ball inside the area and hammering a shot into the roof of the net from 10 yards.

37 Manchester City   Barclays Premier League   5 Oct 2008
With City leading 2-0, Torres got ahead of his marker to steer Alvaro Arbeloa's cross over the line from close-range early in the second half.

38 Manchester City Barclays Premier League   5 Oct 2008
The Spanish striker then drew Liverpool FC level when he met Steven Gerrard's corner with a near-post run and thumping header before Dirk Kuyt completed the comeback with an injury-time winner.

39 Preston North End   FA Cup third round   3 Jan 2009
Steven Gerrard burst clear before sliding the ball across goal to give Torres the simple task of tapping in to an empty net from close-range.

40 Chelsea   Barclays Premier League   1 Feb 2009
Torres sent Anfield wild with two late goals to clinch a 2-0 victory over Chelsea for Liverpool FC. His first came in the 89th minute as the striker got in front of defender Alex to head Fabio Aurelio's centre from the left past Petr Cech.

41 Chelsea
Barclays Premier League 1 Feb 2009
Nando's second arrived just moments later. Yossi Benayoun stole possession from Ashley Cole on the edge of the area before squaring for Torres to tap-home from 10 yards.

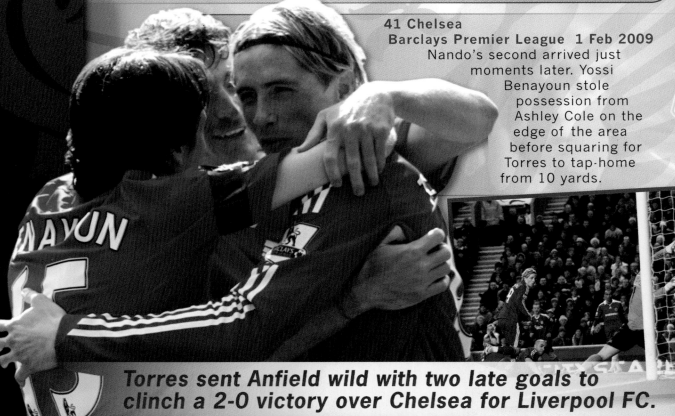

Torres sent Anfield wild with two late goals to clinch a 2-0 victory over Chelsea for Liverpool FC.

42 Portsmouth   Barclays Premier League   7 Feb 2009
Yossi Benayoun collected possession inside the left edge of the area and the Israeli delivered a pin-point centre, which was met by a bullet header from the Reds' number nine that left Pompey stopper David James helpless.

43 Real Madrid   Champions League last 16 (2nd leg)   10 Mar 2009
After a vigorous opening, the Spanish international netted after 16 minutes. Jamie Carragher's long-ball forward was allowed to bounce by Real defender Pepe, allowing Dirk Kuyt to square for Torres to steer beyond Iker Casillas from six yards.

44 Manchester United   Barclays Premier League   14 Mar 2009
The Liverpool FC number nine forced Nemanja Vidic into misjudging Martin Skrtel's long-ball and the Spanish international used his strength to hold off the United centre-back before clinically slipping a low shot into the bottom corner when one-on-one with Edwin van der Sar.

45 Chelsea   Champions League quarter-final (1st leg)   8 Apr 2009
Dirk Kuyt back-heeled the ball into the path of Alvaro Arbeloa's marauding run and he crossed for his Spanish international team-mate to steer a controlled drive past Petr Cech from 12-yards.

46 Blackburn Rovers
Barclays Premier League 11 Apr 2009
Jamie Carragher's flighted ball forward was controlled on the chest by Torres, before he swivelled and sent an unstoppable volley over the despairing arms of Paul Robinson in an instant.

47 Blackburn Rovers
Barclays Premier League
11 Apr 2009
Nando claimed his second of an emphatic afternoon as he evaded his marker to score with a header from Xabi Alonso's pin-point free-kick.

48 Arsenal
Barclays Premier League
21 Apr 2009
The 25-year-old rose highest to meet Dirk Kuyt's cross and plant an unstoppable header beyond the reach of Gunners' goalie Lukasz Fabianski.

49 Arsenal
Barclays Premier League 21 Apr 2009
Collecting the ball with his back to goal, Torres created half a yard of space for himself against Mikael Silvestre before guiding a low shot into the bottom corner.

50 Tottenham Hotspur
Barclays Premier League 24 May 2009
The final day of the season... not that much to play for.. but don't tell that to El Nino as the Spanish striker placed a brilliant header past Gomes in the Tottenham goal from Dirk Kuyt's deep right wing cross.

Ahead of the kick-off to the brand new season, the Liverpool FC squad spent a week in Asia where they entertained their vast armies of supporters in Thailand and Singapore.

It was a week when pre-season preparation was combined with a range of commercial activities, as the Reds went out and about to meet their faraway fans.

Here are some of the best pictures from a memorable week, which included training, competitive football, coaching clinics and a boat ride.

Dirk Kuyt

Dirk Kuyt penned a new Anfield deal at the end of last season - and then spoke of his desire to start building a medal collection with the Reds.

The hard-working Dutchman saw his excellent form rewarded with a new contract, but despite feeling elation at his club's desire for him to remain on Merseyside, he insists the time has come for the Reds to pick up more silverware. And having not yet picked up a winners medal during his time at the club, he's desperate to right that statistic this year.

"I am really pleased to have agreed the deal," he said. "It was a dream come true when I signed for the club and it's great to know I will be involved in any successes we have over the next three years.

"Liverpool is one of the biggest clubs in the world and to know they wanted me to stay is fantastic. Last season we really showed what we are capable of and I'm looking forward to helping us to keep moving forward.

"If we keep working as hard as possible I am confident we can enjoy success together over the coming years.

"We've got great quality in our team and there's no reason why in the future we can't win a lot of trophies together. That's our aim."

For manager Rafael Benitez, the decision to offer Kuyt a new Liverpool FC deal was among the easiest he has made during his time at the helm.

"Dirk had one year left on his contract and we were keen for him to stay. He is a player with great quality who has a big part to play in our future. We are delighted to have reached an agreement.

"There are not many better clubs than Liverpool. I've been here for almost three years and I've had a great time, playing with the best players in the world."

"When you talk about Dirk you are talking about a fantastic professional, a fantastic player and a nice person. You always know you will get one hundred per cent from him and the work he does for the team is unbelievable.

"When we look ahead to our future it is clear Dirk will be a part of it. He has quality, intelligence, he doesn't mind where he is asked to play for the good of the team and he can score goals. He scored 15 last season which was a good total.

"The fans can appreciate what he brings to the side. He never stops running, never stops working and I am so pleased we can look forward to him being at the club for at least another three years."

"It was a dream come true when I signed for the club and it's great to know I will be involved in any successes we have over the next three years."

As well as being thrilled with his own deal, Kuyt was pleased to hear of Rafa Benitez and Steven Gerrard also putting pen to paper - with a settled squad very much key to any chance the Reds have of glory.

"I think it's important for Stevie and the manager to have extended their contracts because they are vital to the club," he added.

"I'm really happy with my own contract and I think there will be a few more players to follow us, which is good because we have a great team and I hope we can win a lot of trophies together.

"There are not many better clubs than Liverpool. I've been here for almost three years and I've had a great time, playing with the best players in the world.

"Once you sign for Liverpool, you want to stay here as long as possible.

"This team is getting better and better and I think the most important thing is we have spent a long period playing with each other.

"Most of the players have played with each other for a few years now and that is really positive.

"We have made a lot of progress. We've shown we can beat the best, even in the most difficult of situations. We've proven we can compete with the other top teams."

New Academy Director Frank McParland explains the philosophy behind Liverpool Football Club's desire to develop stars of the future at their Kirkby-based complex.

"At the Liverpool FC Academy we have one simple aim - to produce footballers of the future by nurturing the natural talent of youngsters from Merseyside and beyond. Where there is ability we want to get the best out of it; where there is talent we want to harness it and where there is desire we want to reward it with opportunity.

"Our determination to give young players of genuine potential the chance to make it in one of the toughest and most competitive sports is such that we aim to provide every single youngster who walks through our doors with the best of everything - the best coaching, the best facilities and the best possible guidance.

"The Academy is an integral part of the club and this means everyone who works, trains and plays here is expected to perform to the highest possible standards. Our ongoing challenge is to provide the ideal environment for talent to flourish and it is one which we endeavour to meet on a daily basis.

"We are only too well aware that in order to produce the best players you need to have the best staff and this is why we have brought in some of the finest available coaching talent from home and abroad.

"In recruiting Kenny Dalglish - a Liverpool Football Club legend as player and manager - and internationally renowned youth coach Jose Segura we have ensured that we are living up to our aim of giving our youngsters the very best.

"Kenny needs no introduction to fans of this club or football in general and while Jose may not be as well known in this part of the world his reputation for helping develop stars of the future of the calibre of Andres Iniesta, Cesc Fabregas, Mikel Arteta and Gerard Pique makes him a hugely valuable addition to our staff.

"The Academy is a special place; one where dreams are fired, hopes are heightened and aspirations are raised."

"We feel that the additions of Kenny and Jose will prove invaluable to our youngsters both in the short term and the long term. The Academy is a special place; one where dreams are fired, hopes are heightened and aspirations are raised. It is also the first rung on the ladder that could lead to a career with Liverpool Football Club."

Kenny Dalglish on returning to Liverpool FC

"I spoke to Rafa a few months ago and things have progressed from there. Now that it has come to fruition I am very excited, but also a bit nervous.

"For the boss to put his trust in me is a great compliment and I am coming back as a very lucky person. When you leave a club you don't often have a chance to return, so I am fortunate for being given such a fantastic opportunity.

"Rafa has made a very brave decision to revamp the Academy. There are lots of positive things happening here and there is a real feel-good factor around the place. It's fantastic for me to be a part of that.

"People who come to the Academy should be delighted that Rafa is taking such an interest in the development of the young players. Everyone knows the most important team at the club is the first team and hopefully we can start producing players to challenge for a place in Rafa's plans. It won't happen overnight but I'm looking forward to working with Frank McParland and the rest of the Academy staff to do the best job I can."

Rafael Benitez on Kenny's return

"I am really pleased to have Kenny as a part of the staff. We were looking for someone who has a knowledge of and a passion for the club and Kenny is the perfect choice.

"He will help at the Academy with the development of players and will also have an ambassadorial role at the club. If you're looking for somebody to go around the world on behalf of Liverpool Football Club then I don't know anybody better than Kenny.

"When you talk to him about players and football systems it's clear he has a lot of experience. That's good for the club and also for the young players coming through.

"We are changing things at the Academy, we are bringing in new ideas and new people but we're keeping the spirit and the heart of the club. Kenny has played for the club, he's managed the club, he's done everything. He's a fantastic signing."

Glen Johnson

Glen, there was reportedly interest from other clubs, so why did you choose Liverpool FC?

Because it's a fantastic club and, to be honest, I've always had a soft spot for Liverpool, so it was an easy decision to make.

Your affinity for Liverpool FC all started from the first kit you had when you were a boy, didn't it?

Yes, when I was a young boy all I ever wanted to do was play football and I used to run around my garden in my Liverpool kit, which was the first kit my mum ever bought for me. Living in south London I don't know where that came from, but I guess everything happens for a reason.

What can you achieve at Liverpool FC?

I want to do as well as I can and try and help the team improve. The lads had a fantastic season last year finishing second and everyone in the squad is now looking to improve on that. There are some fantastic names in this squad, the likes of Steven Gerrard, Fernando Torres and so on. It's going to be brilliant for me to play alongside players like that.

Rafa Benitez has obviously spent a lot of money to bring you here. What can you add to Liverpool FC?

I don't know really, I guess you'll have to wait and see. People saw my game last season and I'd like to think I can do the same here with a bit more added.

The move to Chelsea didn't really work out for you though, did it? What do you put that down to?

When I first went to Chelsea things were going fine. I was 18 and playing in all of the games I was available for under Claudio Ranieri. So things started well, but when Jose Mourinho came in, he had different ideas and brought his own players in and, for whatever reason, it didn't work out for me. So I made a choice and decided to leave.

Do you feel your career has gone full circle now?

Yes. I left Chelsea for a reason and I'm glad I was able to achieve that at Portsmouth, but obviously I won't be resting on my laurels. I want to push on again.

You picked up a Premier League winners' medal with Chelsea. You probably didn't play as many games as you would have liked, but can you use any of that experience here at Liverpool FC?

Definitely. Chelsea were obviously a fantastic side and did well to win the league. I may not have played as many games as I would have liked to, but there's no point in worrying about the past because I want to make the most of the future. I will just use the experience and take it with me.

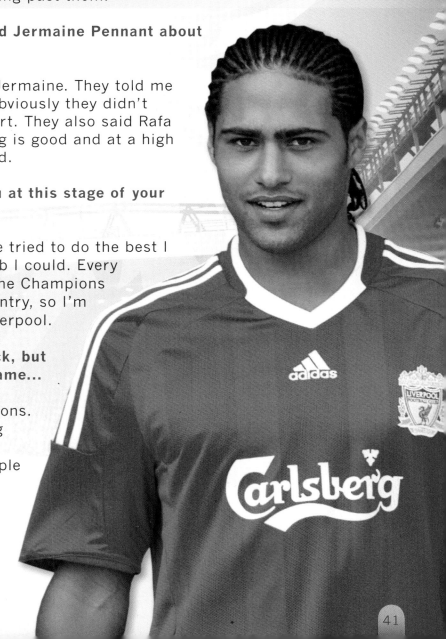

You must believe this Liverpool FC side can win the Premier League?

Yes, definitely. They went so close to doing it last season and the lads have so much desire to improve and get that medal. I would not put anything past them.

Did you ask Peter Crouch and Jermaine Pennant about life at Anfield?

Yes, I spoke to Crouchy and Jermaine. They told me this is a fantastic club, but obviously they didn't really need to tell me that part. They also said Rafa is a nice man and the training is good and at a high intensity, which is what I need.

Is this the right move for you at this stage of your career?

In every game I've played I've tried to do the best I could to play for the best club I could. Every player's dream is to play in the Champions League and play for your country, so I'm over the moon to come to Liverpool.

Fans know you as a right-back, but there is versatility to your game...

Yes, I can play in other positions. Funnily enough, I was playing just behind the front two for Portsmouth in their final couple of games last season, but I think that was just a one off!

41

Alberto Aquilani

Alberto Aquilani has revealed how a chat with former Red John Arne Riise convinced him to swap Italy for Merseyside.

Aquilani signed in at Anfield during the summer after a lengthy career with AS Roma - and he admits Riise played no small part in helping him to choose a new career path.

"Obviously I am a friend of Riise's and he's spoken a lot about Liverpool to me," Aquilani told reporters at his unveiling on Thursday. "I've spoken to him about the Kop and the great fans and I can't wait to start.

"I have never played at Anfield but I have heard a lot about the unique atmosphere you breathe there.

"Rafa Benitez was very important in me coming here. Riise spoke very well of him and said he could help me grow as a player.

"I was already aware and appreciated his work even before the opportunity arose to come here. I like the way the team plays and certainly it was a deciding factor.

"I'm very proud Rafa chose me. I also want to thank (chief scout) Eduardo Macia, who was very important."

Aquilani faced a frustrating start to his Liverpool FC career after being sidelined with an ankle injury, but he admits he was always relishing the prospect of playing alongside some of the best players in the world.

"I think the Premier League is the most difficult. It's one of the best leagues and there are some very important teams here. It's a very difficult level but I'm very excited to be playing here.

"It's a team of good players and has been for some years now," he said. "I have always liked the system of play here and the players. Even before coming here I thought Gerrard was the strongest midfielder in the world.

"I am very proud that I will be playing alongside him and I hope I can learn from him.

"I think the Premier League is the most difficult. It's one of the best leagues and there are some very important teams here. It's a very difficult level but I'm very excited to be playing here.

"We're definitely one of the candidates to win the Premier League."

Our new number four was also keen to emphasise he shouldn't be seen as a natural replacement for Xabi Alonso.

"I hope I am going to play an important role," he said. "The manager obviously knows my characteristics and strong points and I hope to be able to fulfil all the hope he has in me.

"I am the kind of midfielder who moves around a lot. I try to combine quality with movement. I am not a static player - I move around a lot and I think this is one of my strengths.

"Xabi was very important here and I'm not his natural substitute. I don't have the exact same characteristics he has. He was very important here and I hope I can be similarly important."

He added: "Everyone knows a lot about the history of Liverpool. It's world famous and not just because they have won five European Cups," said the Italy international.

"I grew up in Rome and the final with Roma was something I was very much aware of. You can't ignore the huge past this club has.

"I am very pleased. This is an important occasion for me. I'm here at a big club and I'm very happy to be here.

"I say this because Liverpool is among the strongest in the world with very important history."

Study the picture below closely, then use your skill to spot where you think the ball might be.

Answer P.61

Study the two pictures below closely, then try to spot the 9 differences between them.

YOU'LL NEVER WALK ALONE

LIVERPOOL
FOOTBALL CLUB

EST·1892

Daniel Agger

Daniel Agger has revealed he had no hesitation in putting pen to paper on a new Liverpool FC contract - even though there have been no guarantees over first team football.

The classy Danish defender's future had been the subject of much speculation over many months, with top clubs from abroad rumoured to be interested in taking him from Anfield.

But any doubts over where his heart was were set aside at the back end of last season when he announced Liverpool FC is the only club he wants to play for.

The Dane accepted a new five-year deal last month despite having to settle for 26 senior appearances in 2008/09.

And Agger has revealed how Benitez made no promises about when he would play.

"First of all, I believe this team, with the players we have, will be able to challenge for many honours and trophies over the next few years," Agger explained.

"Secondly, I think I have a chance to play in this team, otherwise I would not be staying at the club.

"Thirdly, I really like this city, and I like the people who live here. It's not the same as my home town, Copenhagen, but I actually really like where I live. That's important.

"I believe if you have a happy, settled and comfortable life outside the pitch then you're going to be a much better player on it."

Agger added: "Of course, if you have a manager who tells you that he is confident in your ability and he believes in you and what you can bring to the team, then that is also important. The manager has done this by coming to me and offering me the contract.

"In football you can't get any promises from the manager about when you are going to play, and especially not at a club like Liverpool where we have so many talented players all competing for places.

"I believe I am good enough to play regularly in this team and that's what I want to do."

Having arrived at Anfield during the club's 2006 FA Cup triumph, Agger is still waiting for his first winner's medal as a Liverpool FC player. And he is confident it won't be too long before he tastes glory.

"Everybody wants medals, they want trophies and they want success," he said. "That is what a club like Liverpool should be all about.

"I believe this team, with the players we have, will be able to challenge for many honours and trophies over the next few years."

"I won both the league and cup in my first season at Brondby. I haven't won anything at Liverpool so far and that is something I really want to change.

"We won the FA Cup in my first season at the club but I didn't play a game in the competition that season. So although I have a medal for that victory I don't count it as my having won it.

"I think you can see on the pitch this season, and especially in the last few games, what playing for this club means for the team.

"We have showed that we have a winning character now throughout the team. We have developed this season a mentality which says that you can't beat us.

"Even when we are in a difficult position we have a belief in our ability to change the result."

Rafa on Agger

"It's fantastic news that Daniel has committed his future to Liverpool. He is a young player who is improving all the time and whose best years are clearly ahead of him.

"He is an excellent defender but also gives us different options with the ball as he is good at coming out and using it well. At home in particular this can be helpful for us against sides who look to defend in numbers.

"We wanted him to stay and he wanted to stay so we are all pleased we were able to do the deal."

Appearances

Ian Callaghan

Most first team appearances	Ian Callaghan (857)
Most League appearances	Ian Callaghan (640)
Most FA Cup appearances	Ian Callaghan (79)
Most League Cup appearances	Ian Rush (78)
Most European appearances	Jamie Carragher (116)
Oldest player	Ted Doig, 41 yrs & 165 days v Newcastle United (A) 11 April 1908
Youngest player	Max Thompson, 17 yrs & 129 days v Tottenham Hotspur (A) 8 May 1974
Most seasons as an ever-present	Phil Neal (9)
Most consecutive appearances	Phil Neal (417) 23 October 1976 to 24 Sept. 1983
Longest serving player	Elisha Scott · 21 yrs & 52 days (1913 to 1934)
Oldest debutant	Ted Doig, 37 yrs & 307 days v Burton U (H) 1 Sept. 1904

Goals

Most first team goals	Ian Rush (346)
Most League goals	Roger Hunt (245)
Most FA Cup goals	Ian Rush (39)
Most League Cup goals	Ian Rush (48)
Most European goals	Steven Gerrard (32)
Highest scoring sub	David Fairclough (18)
Most hat-tricks	Gordon Hodgson (17)
Most hat-tricks in a season	Roger Hunt (5 in 1961-62)
Most penalties scored	Jan Molby (42)
Most games without scoring	Ephraim Longworth (371)
Youngest goalscorer	Michael Owen, 17 yrs & 144 days v Wimbledon (A) 6 May 1997
Oldest goalscorer	Billy Liddell, 38 yrs & 55 days v Stoke City (H) 5 March 1960

Elisha Scott

Billy Liddell

Internationals

Most capped player
Steven Gerrard (74) with England

Most international goals
Ian Rush (26) with Wales
Michael Owen (26) with England

Michael Owen

Honours

Most medals Phil Neal (20)

Phil Neal

Matches

Record victory 11-0 v Strømsgodset
Record defeat 1-9 v Birmingham City

Transfer Fees

Record transfer fee paid Fernando Torres
Record transfer fee received Xabi Alonso

Attendances

Highest League attendance 58,757 v Chelsea, 1949/50

Highest FA Cup attendance 61,905 v Wolves, 1951/52 fifth round

Highest League Cup attendance 50,880 v Nottingham Forest, 1979/80 semi-final 2nd leg

v Nottingham Forest 27 Jan 1980

Highest European attendance 55,104 v Barcelona, 1975/76 UEFA Cup semi-final 2nd leg

Lowest League attendance 1,000 v Loughborough Town on 7 December 1895

Lowest League attendance (post-war) 11,976 v Scunthorpe United for a Division 2 game, 22 April 1959

Lowest FA Cup attendance 4,000 v Newton on 29 October 1892 2nd Qualifying Rd

Lowest FA Cup attendance (post-war) 11,207 v Chester City, 1945/46 3rd rd 2nd leg

Lowest League Cup attendance 9,902 v Brentford, 1983/84 2nd rd, 2nd leg

Lowest European attendance 12,021 v Dundalk, 1982/83 European Cup 1st rd, 1st leg

Record highest attendance 61,905 v Wolves, 1951/52 FA Cup fifth round

Record lowest attendance 1,000 v Loughborough Town on 7 December 1895

Correct to end of 2008/09 Season

Pepe Reina may have earned himself a reputation as an expert for keeping clean sheets over recent seasons - but he happily admits he would swap shut-outs if it meant trophies coming back to Anfield.

The Liverpool FC goalkeeper just missed out on the Golden Glove award last time after winning it for each of the previous three seasons.

But the amiable Spaniard insists silverware and not personal glory is the only motivation which drives him forward on a daily basis.

"Of course I'd swap the lot," Reina said. "I had a little challenge going with Petr Cech last season where we'd see who could concede the least goals.

"Despite our club rivalries we're both in the goalkeepers' union! We'd send text messages to each other about the clean sheets as well. I told him I would swap all my clean sheets for his league titles.

"All we want here at Liverpool is to win the Premier League. I'd prefer to win every game 3-2 if it meant we won the title at the end of the season.

"It would have been nice to win the Golden Glove award again, even if it meant sharing the award with Van der Sar.

"It is always nice to keep records though. In my case that means conceding as few goals as possible.

"Other than when we beat United 4-1 at Old Trafford, Van der Sar has been brilliant.

"He is well worth the Golden Glove award so congratulations to him. At one point he was part of an amazing run in which he kept 14 consecutive clean sheets. What more can I say?

"I remember keeping 11 consecutive clean sheets in my first year with Liverpool. That was in all competitions though, so maybe just six or seven in the Premier League. It was still a good record but 14 in the league is also impressive."

He may have firmly established himself as one of the best goalkeepers in the game with his performances between the Liverpool FC sticks over recent seasons, but he still baulks at suggestions he should be compared to Ray Clemence · arguably the Reds' finest ever number one.

"You will hear people talking about different eras and likening successful sides of the past to successful teams of the present," he added.

"I'm not sure it's fair to do that. I'm not even sure what system Liverpool used when Clemence played or whether teams were attacking more or less than they do today.

"There are so many things that you have to consider.

"All we want here at Liverpool is to win the Premier League. I'd prefer to win every game 3-2 if it meant we won the title at the end of the season."

"What I do know is that Clemence was probably the best goalkeeper in Liverpool's history. Of course, my aim is to achieve just half of what Clemence did with Liverpool. If I manage that it will be a successful time for the club."

He added: "I appreciate all the nice things people have said about me.

"I feel I have improved many things in my game during the four years I have been at Liverpool. But I still have plenty of things to clear and am still young in terms of being a goalkeeper.

"I am only 26 so still have a pretty long way to go. Hopefully that will be with Liverpool."

1. "Some people believe football is a matter of life and death, I am very disappointed with that attitude. I can assure you it is much, much more important than that." Bill Shankly

2. "If Everton were playing at the bottom of the garden, I'd pull the curtains." Bill Shankly

3. "The trouble with referees is that they know the rules, but they don't know the game." Bill Shankly

4. "A lot of football success is in the mind. You must believe that you are the best and then make sure that you are. In my time at Liverpool we always said we had the best two teams in Merseyside, Liverpool and Liverpool reserves." Bill Shankly

5. "If you're in the penalty area and don't know what to do with the ball, put it in the net and we'll discuss the options later." Bob Paisley

6. "Liverpool was made for me and I was made for Liverpool." Bill Shankly

7. "Liverpool without European football is like a banquet without wine." Roy Evans

8. "Mind you, I've been here during the bad times too · one year we came second." Bob Paisley

9. "I hate talking about football. I just do it, you know?" Robbie Fowler

10. "Sometimes I feel I'm hardly wanted in this Liverpool team. If I get two or three saves to make, I've had a busy day." Ray Clemence

11. "Anyone who doesn't learn from Ian Rush needs shooting." Robbie Fowler

12. "Liverpool are magic, Everton are tragic." Emlyn Hughes

13. "I'd kick my own brother if necessary... it's what being a professional footballer is all about." Steve McMahon

14. "It was like playing in a foreign country." Ian Rush on his time with Juventus

15. "I said to Kevin (Keegan), 'I'll go near post' and he replied, 'No, just go for the ball.'" Tommy Smith

16. "Anybody who plays for me should be a bad loser." Graeme Souness.

17. "It's best being a striker. If you miss five then score the winner, you're a hero. The goalkeeper can play a blinder, then let one in... and he's a villain." Ian Rush

18. "Of course I didn't take my wife to see Rochdale as an anniversary present, it was her birthday. Would I have got married in the football season? Anyway, it was Rochdale reserves." Bill Shankly

19. "They compare Steve McManaman to Steve Heighway and he's nothing like him, but I can see why - it's because he's a bit different." Kevin Keegan

20. "Bruce Grobbelaar will play on until he is 40 - and at the top level." Bruce Grobbelaar

21. "He's better than Brian Lara because he's 600 not out. What a guy." Roy Evans on Ian Rush's 600th appearance for Liverpool FC

22. "Should the aggregate score be level after 90 minutes, extra time will be played." Fulham's matchday programme for the 2nd leg of the Littlewoods Cup tie in 1986/87. Liverpool FC were 10-0 up from the first leg

23. "There are those who say maybe I should forget about football. Maybe I should forget about breathing." Gerard Houllier

24. "Nobody likes being criticised, particularly by players who will be in Disneyland this summer on their holidays rather than the World Cup in Japan." Phil Thompson responding to Frank de Boer of Barcelona who said Liverpool FC were boring

Bill Shankly

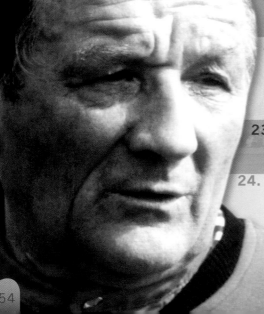

Bob Paisley

25. "Son, you'll do well here as long as you remember two things. Don't over-eat and don't lose your accent." Bill Shankly to Ian St John

26. "If you are first you are first. If you are second you are nothing." Bill Shankly

27. "Don't worry Alan. At least you'll be able to play close to a great team!" Bill Shankly to Alan Ball after he signed for Everton

28. "Shanks was the father figure but Roger Hunt was something special. It might sound daft but just picking up his sweaty kit gave me satisfaction." Phil Thompson

29. "As Arnold Schwarzenegger said, 'I'll be back.'" Gerard Houllier

30. "There is no way the second half can be as entertaining as the first." Alan Hansen during the UEFA Cup Final v Alaves with Liverpool FC leading 3-1 at half-time

31. "We don't have any splits here. The players country is Liverpool Football Club and their language is football." Gerard Houllier

32. "It's there to remind our lads who they're playing for, and to remind the opposition who they're playing against." Bill Shankly about the 'This is Anfield' plaque

Kenny Dalglish

33. "Just go out and drop a few hand grenades all over the place son." Bill Shankly to Kevin Keegan

34. "It broke my heart to leave Liverpool." Kenny Dalglish

35. "Ay, here we are with problems at the top of the league." Bill Shankly suggesting to a journalist that Liverpool FC were in difficulties

36. "Where are you from?" "I'm a Liverpool fan from London." "Well laddie, what's it like to be in heaven?" Bill Shankly to a Liverpool FC fan

37. "Yes Roger Hunt misses a few, but he gets in the right place to miss them." Bill Shankly to a reporter

38. "With him in defence, we could play Arthur Askey in goal." Bill Shankly after signing Ron Yeats

39. "Steve Nicol never gives more than 120 per cent." Kevin Keegan

40. "At Liverpool we never accept second best." Kenny Dalglish

41. "Bill was so strong it was unbelievable. You couldn't shake him off the ball. It didn't matter where he was playing, though I suppose his best position was outside-left. He could go round you, or past you, or even straight through you sometimes!" Bob Paisley on Billy Liddell

42. "We will beat them one day, I can promise you that!" Gerard Houllier on Manchester United

43. "If anybody thinks either myself or my team are afraid of Liverpool, they can think again. I believe I've got a team that can go out and do the business against them." Coventry manager John Sillett before a match with Liverpool FC in 1987. Liverpool FC won 4-1 with Sillett declaring them champions elect in August.

44. "You can't build a cathedral in a day. A look at the club's history tells you these things take time." Gerard Houllier

45. Barnes did what we expected him to do. He made a goal, scored one, and entertained. You remember that." Kenny Dalglish after John Barnes Anfield debut for Liverpool FC in a 2-0 win over Oxford in 1987

46. "He couldn't play anyway. I only wanted him for the reserve team!" Bill Shankly upon hearing Celtic's Lou Macari had snubbed Liverpool FC in favour of a move to Manchester United.

47. "Laddie, I never drop players, I only make changes." Bill Shankly to a journalist who criticised his team selection

48. "I don't believe everything Bill tells me about his players. Had they been that good, they'd not only have won the European Cup but the Ryder Cup, the Boat Race and even the Grand National!" Celtic manager Jock Stein on Bill Shankly

49. "We've got a lot of Cockneys in the team, but really, it doesn't matter where they're from - we're all playing for Liverpool." Robbie Fowler

Ian Rush

50. "It's great grass at Anfield, professional grass!" Bill Shankly comparing the Anfield pitch to other grounds.

Albert Riera believes Liverpool FC must enjoy an almost error-free campaign if they are to have a chance of tasting success this season.

The Reds' Spanish midfielder is confident there is enough quality in the squad to mount another serious title charge this time around, but he knows from experience how costly mistakes at crucial times of the season can ultimately prove to be.

"Last year the winner had 90 points, that means you cannot have a lot of mistakes," he said. "You need to win every single game.

"Our mistakes last year were at Anfield, when we made three draws in a row and we lost six points. We cannot lose those points again."

Riera has enjoyed an impressive start to his Liverpool FC career since swapping La Liga for Merseyside last summer, but he insists there is still much more to come from him as he continues to adapt to the English game.

"I always think I can be better, but I think for my first season at Anfield I did okay," he added.

"It's never easy for a player moving to a new club. Adapting wasn't as difficult for me because I'd been in England before. I can improve and I have to. I know that and I will be trying to do that in the new season.

"The Champions League and Premier League are massive and I enjoy taking part in them.

"The fact that we had some terrific results against good opponents obviously helps.

"I realised straight away when I came here that the mentality was different to what I'd experienced. It is a winning attitude and that means pressure is no problem for us,"

"We did well against United, Chelsea, Arsenal and Real Madrid, home and away.

"The only real disappointment in those big games came when we faced Chelsea at home in the European Cup.

"Apart from that, the other results show that we are a good team and are ready to fight for the title.

"We were able to go away from home against top sides and do well. That's what you need."

And Riera also admits the belief within the Reds squad has given him the confidence to believe 'number 19' might not be too far away.

"I realised straight away when I came here that the mentality was different to what I'd experienced. It is a winning attitude and that means pressure is no problem for us," he said.

"I think you always have to improve, all of us. You do that by working harder. I'm sure we will all be doing exactly that."

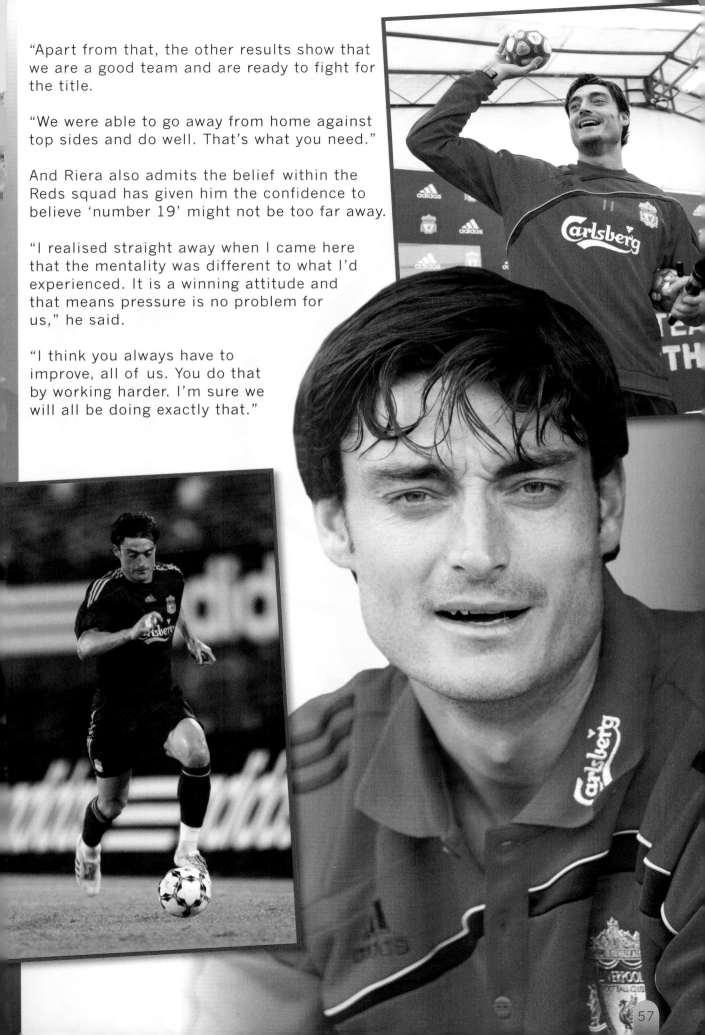

Brazilian star Lucas insists piling on the pounds will aid his bid to establish himself as a Premier League midfielder.

The Liverpool FC star has had to play understudy in the Reds midfield during his time on Merseyside to date, but he hasn't lost his appetite to force his way into becoming a regular part of Rafael Benitez's plans. And he believes adding weight to his slender frame can only help his bid to prove his undoubted quality at Anfield.

"I gained some weight last season and that has helped me be more prepared to play with the demands you face in England," he said.

"I have gained four kilos since I arrived and that's a lot. In my first season, being very honest, I had a problem with physical games.

"Last season, with the extra weight, I felt I could challenge anyone physically and go from one box to the other like I did in Brazil.

"Maybe it has taken me 18 months to get my body physically into the shape that it needed to be in to play my best in England, but I feel that it is coming now for me and I am excited about my future prospects at Liverpool."

Despite improving as last season progressed, Lucas admits he struggled in the early months as the demands of playing in the Olympic Games took hold.

"I missed a lot of the pre-season last time with Liverpool because I was away at the Olympics with Brazil," he explained.

"That meant that I started the pre-season, then I went away, and when I came back to the club it was hard to catch up. I had missed a lot of the important work that the boys all did together.

"Next season I will be here for the whole of the pre-season programme and I believe that will help me play to the very best of my ability."

He added: "As an individual player I feel that I have become a better player, definitely.

"Everyone has bad days at the office when they feel that maybe they haven't played to 100 per cent of what they are capable of.

"I have had those days, too. Of course I have because we all have them.

"But through that I have made progress mentally and physically.

"It was hard at times, but it will all be helpful for me in the long term.

"You get better through the hard times and not through the easy or good times. It gave me a challenge and I think I was able to rise to that.

"I knew I had the quality to be playing in this team, even through the difficult moments. I had the confidence of the manager and the players and even if some supporters were not sure I knew that others were behind me.

"Mentally I'm a better player. I've had the tough times and I've coped well with it and come through the other side."

Quiz Answers

From page 18

1 Atletico Madrid

2 25

3 Tottenham Hotspur

4 Sami Hyypia

5 Brazilian

6 1892

7 Gerard Houllier

8 Bruges

9 Paris

10 Carlsberg

11 Gremio

12 24

13 John McMahon

14 Frank McParland

15 Finnish

16 23

17 PSV Eindhoven

18 Fernando Torres

19 Tottenham Hotspur

20 Fernando Torres v Blackburn

SPOT THE BALL
From page 46

SPOT THE DIFFERENCE
From page 47

YOU'LL NEVER WALK ALONE

LIVERPOOL
FOOTBALL CLUB

EST·1892